Richmond Public Library

<u>D A T E   D U E</u>

POKOT

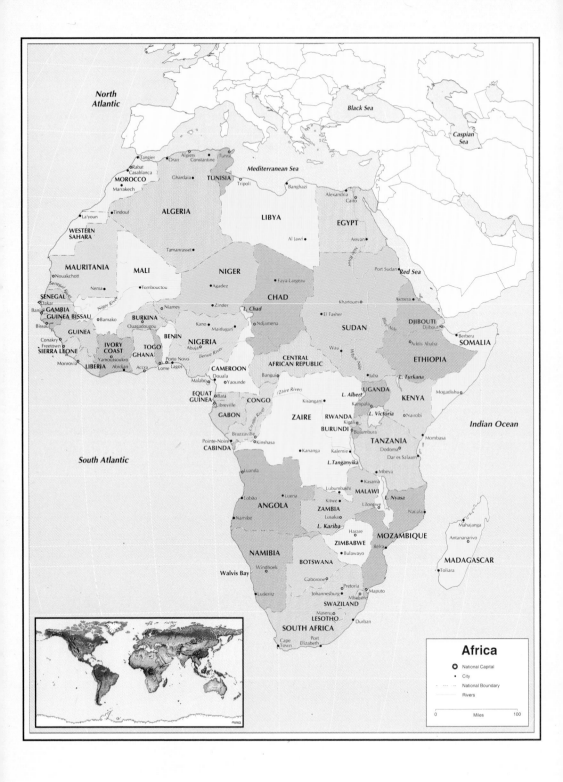

North
Atlantic

Black Sea

Caspian
Sea

Tangier
Algiers Constantine Tunis
Oran
Rabat
Casablanca
MOROCCO
Ghardaia TUNISIA
Tripoli
Mediterranean Sea
Banghazi
Alexandria
Cairo
Marrakech

La'youn
WESTERN
SAHARA
Tindouf
ALGERIA
LIBYA
EGYPT
Al Jawf
Aswan

Nouakchott
MAURITANIA
MALI
NIGER
CHAD
Faya-Largeau
Port Sudan
Red Sea
Asmera

Nema
Tombouctou
Agadez
Khartoum
DJIBOUTI
Djibouti

Senegal River
Dakar
SENEGAL
GAMBIA
Banjul
GUINEA BISSAU
Bissau
GUINEA
Niger River
Niamey
Zinder
L. Chad
Ndjamena
El Fasher
SUDAN
Berbera
SOMALIA

Bamako
BURKINA
Ouagadougou
Kano
Maiduguri
Wau
Addis Ababa
ETHIOPIA

Conakry
Freetown
SIERRA LEONE
BENIN
NIGERIA
Abuja
CENTRAL
AFRICAN REPUBLIC
White Nile
Blue Nile
L. Turkana
Mogadishu

IVORY
COAST
Yamoussoukro
TOGO
GHANA
Porto Novo
Lome Lagos
Benue River
Banqui
Juba

LIBERIA
Monrovia
Abidjan
Accra
CAMEROON
Douala
Yaounde
(Zaire River)
Kisangani
UGANDA
L. Albert
Kampala
KENYA
Nairobi

Malabo
EQUAT.
GUINEA
Bata
Libreville
CONGO
GABON
Congo River
ZAIRE
RWANDA
Kigali
BURUNDI
Bujumbura
L. Victoria
TANZANIA
Mombasa

Brazzaville
Pointe-Noire
Kinshasa
CABINDA
Kananga
Kalemie
Dodoma
Dar es Salaam
L.Tanganyika

Luanda
Lubumbashi
Mbeya
Kasama
MALAWI
L. Nyasa

Lobito
Luena
Kitwe
ZAMBIA
Lusaka
Lilongwe
Nacala

ANGOLA
L. Kariba
MOZAMBIQUE
Mahajanga

Namibe
Harare
ZIMBABWE
Bulawayo
Beira
Antananarivo

South Atlantic
NAMIBIA
BOTSWANA
Windhoek
MADAGASCAR
Toliara

Walvis Bay
Gaborone
Pretoria
Maputo

Luderitz
Johannesburg
Mbabane
SWAZILAND

Maseru
LESOTHO
Durban

SOUTH AFRICA
Cape
Town
Port
Elizabeth

Indian Ocean

Africa

⊕ National Capital
• City
-·-·- National Boundary
—— Rivers

0 — Miles — 100

The Heritage Library of African Peoples

POKOT

Ciarunji Chesaina Swinimer, Ph.D.

THE ROSEN PUBLISHING GROUP, INC.
NEW YORK

Published in 1994 by The Rosen Publishing Group, Inc.
29 East 21st Street, New York, NY 10010

First Edition

Manufactured in the United States of America

Library of Congress Cataloging-in-Publication Data

Swinimer, Ciarunji Chesaina.
   Pokot / Ciarunji Chesaina Swinimer. — 1st ed.
      p.   cm. — (The Heritage library of African peoples)
   Includes bibliographical references and index.
   ISBN 0-8239-1756-8
   1. Suk (African people)—History—Juvenile literature.   2. Suk
(African people)—Social life and customs—Juvenile literature.
I. Title.   II. Series.
DT433.545.S85S94   1994
306'.089'965—dc20   94-5071
                                                             CIP
                                                             AC

Contents

INTRODUCTION

THERE IS EVERY REASON FOR US TO KNOW something about Africa and to understand its past and the way of life of its peoples. Africa is a rich continent that has for centuries provided the world with art, culture, labor, wealth, and natural resources. It has vast mineral deposits, fossil fuels, and commercial crops.

But perhaps most important is the fact that fossil evidence indicates that human beings originated in Africa. The earliest traces of human beings and their tools are almost two million years old. Their descendants have migrated throughout the world. To be human is to be of African descent.

The experiences of the peoples who stayed in Africa are as rich and as diverse as of those who established themselves elsewhere. This series of books describes their environment, their modes of subsistence, their relationships, and their customs and beliefs. The books present the variety of languages, histories, cultures, and religions that are to be found on the African continent. They demonstrate the historical link-ages between African peoples and the way contemporary Africa has been affected by European colonial rule.

Africa is large, complex, and diverse. It encompasses an area of more than 11,700,000 square miles. The United States, Europe, and India could fit easily into it. The sheer size is an indication of the continent's great variety in geography, terrain, climate, flora, fauna, peoples, languages, and cultures.

Much of contemporary Africa has been shaped by European colonial rule, industrialization, urbanization, and the demands of a world economic system. For more than seventy years, large regions of Africa were ruled by Great Britain, France, Belgium, Portugal, and Spain. African peoples from various ethnic, linguistic, and cultural backgrounds were brought together to form colonial states.

For decades Africans struggled to gain their independence. It was not until after World War II that the colonial territories became independent African states. Today, almost all of Africa is ruled by Africans. Large numbers of Africans live in modern cities. Rural Africa is also being transformed, and yet its people still engage in many of their age-old customs and beliefs.

Contemporary circumstances and natural events have not always been kind to ordinary Africans. Today, however, new popular social movements and technological innovations pose great promise for future development.

George C. Bond
Institute of African Studies
Columbia University, New York City

The Pokot are a people with a strong and proud heritage.

chapter

1

THE LAND AND THE PEOPLE

A famous Kenyan proverb says:

Whoever does not travel
Outside his home
Thinks that
Only his mother
Knows how to cook.

THESE WISE WORDS APPLY TO ALL OF US WHO are content with only what we know. It applies to people who are narrow-minded and unwilling to explore the lives of people beyond their own town or country. Anyone who has ever been in the Cherangani Hills of western Kenya must have been fascinated by the proud farmers and cattle-herders who have lived there for centuries. The Pokot demand our attention because of the traditional way of life they maintain despite the

The Pokot demand our attention because of the traditional way of life they maintain despite the many pressures of change.

many pressures to change. Although no culture is static, and changes have occurred among the Pokot, their own sense of history and daily life contribute to the richness that is Africa.

▼ THE PEOPLE ▼

The Pokot are approximately 220,000 in number. They have been called Suk or Karasuk, but they have known themselves as Pokot for centuries. The Pokot are dark, tall, and slim.

The Pokot trace their origin to the Nile River Valley. Their closest relatives are the Kipsigis, Keiyo, Marakwet, Nandi, Tugen, and Sebeei. These seven peoples, known as the Kalenjin ethnic group, share a language also called Kalenjin, which means, "I tell you." All Kalenjin speakers can understand each other, but the Pokot language has many variations.

The Pokot are of two main groups: cattle-herders or pastoralists and farmers or agricultur-alists. The pastoralists represent roughly three quarters of the population. In Kalenjin they are called *pipatich*, "cattle people," and the agri-culturalists are called *pipapagh*, "grain people."

▼ THE LAND ▼

The Pokot live in the Upper Rift Valley of western Kenya. Their land is a narrow strip about 145 miles long and 45 miles wide, running northwest to southeast. It is a poor environment.

Pokot agriculturalists are called pipapagh.

The land varies from desert to hot dry plains to cool wet highlands. The rainy season lasts from March to September. Rainfall ranges from 30 to 50 inches a year in the mountainous areas to 10 to 15 inches a year in the plains.

Water is scarce in most of Pokotland. The only large river is the Suam, which flows north into Lake Turkana. Rain is not a frequent visitor to the Pokot, especially in the lowlands that form most of their land.

The most visible features of Pokotland are the hills. The western part is covered by the Cherangani Hills, 10,000 feet above sea level. To

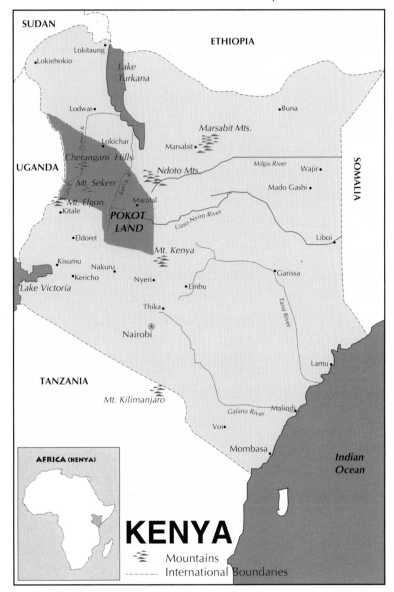

the north is Mount Sekker, 10,910 feet. The rest
of the area is plains, between 2,500 and 5,000
feet above sea level.

Besides heavier rainfall, the mountainous
areas are blessed with black soil. Here are huge

13

TRICKSTER TALE
The Hare and the Elephant

The elephant was walking along the road and met the hare. "Oh, I'm tired and I have blisters," said the hare. "Carry me on your back." So the elephant lifted him up. On his back the elephant was carrying a pot of honey, and the hare ate all of it. Then the hare said, "Hand me some stones. I will throw them at the birds to frighten them away." The elephant handed some stones to the hare, who put them in the empty honeypot. Then the hare said, "Give me some sand so I can wipe the sweat off my face." When the elephant handed him same sand, the hare used it to fill in the stones and make them level. Then he spread a few drops of honey from his paw on top of the sand in the pot, so it looked untouched. The elephant was fooled, and the clever hare got a ride home and a belly full of honey!

cedar trees, bamboo, and grass. The forests in turn help to maintain the plant life by holding rainfall.

Along the river banks the soil is fertile and damp. The river courses are lined with evergreen trees. Among them are wild fig trees that grow as tall as 30 feet. The hardwood of the acacia trees is used as fuel and for carving utensils and

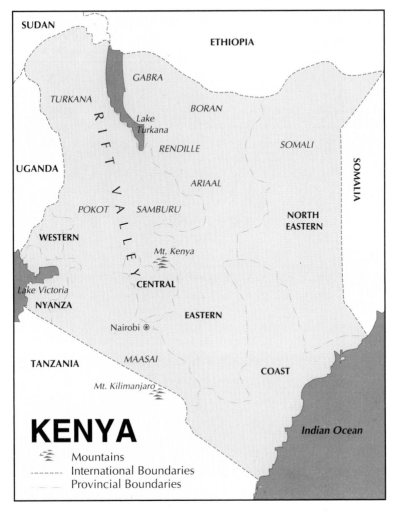

KENYA

- 🏔 Mountains
- ------ International Boundaries
- -·-·- Provincial Boundaries

hoeheads. In contrast, the plains have poor vegetation. Besides low rainfall and extreme heat, the plains have poor red soil that suffers from erosion. Here are found the flowering plant euphorbia and the prickly bush. Some areas of the desert have little or no plant life.

The largest animals found in Pokotland are buffalo, which live in the mountains and the plains. In the forests on mountain slopes and on

15

One of the challenges that the Pokot face is the scarce supply of water in the lowlands.

river courses, colobus monkeys live in the tree-tops. Small antelopes live in the plains. Their hides are used for clothing. Other animals are baboons and wild pigs, which are destructive to crops.

Small birds provide some beauty in this impoverished land. Ostriches, huge desert birds, supply feathers for decorating headgear worn during ceremonies or traditional dances.▲

chapter

2

POLITICS AND SOCIETY

THE POKOT ARE DIVIDED INTO MORE THAN thirty clans, groups of families with a common ancestor. Each clan is identified by a totem animal. The clan system gives the people a point of reference and a basis of communal sharing. For example, in times of famine, a family can depend for assistance on the members of its clan. The clan is thought of as one family. It is taboo for a man to marry a woman from his clan because she is regarded as his sister.

The clans live in homesteads. Each homestead is headed by an elder called the *poion*. A homestead consists of a hut for the *poion* and one for each of his wives and her young children. The Pokot practice polygamy, under which a man can have many wives. The married sons usually build their own huts in the same vicinity, forming an extended family headed by the *poion*.

A Pokot hut.

The *poion* elders are people who have distinguished themselves in the community and amassed large herds of cattle. The *poion*'s character is of great importance. He must be wise and have wide experience in life. The leadership of several homesteads is under a council of elders known as the *kokwa*. The *kokwa* handles communal matters such as sharing of resources and work, settlement of disputes, and maintenance of law and order.

The highest authority among the Pokot today is an elder known as *kiruokintin,* or chief. The *kiruokintin* is accorded high respect for his

Each Pokot homestead is headed by an elder called a *poion*.

wisdom, qualities of leadership, and high sense of justice. Decisions concerning extraordinary events are made under his chairmanship. He also settles disputes that cannot be resolved by the *kokwa*. Despite his heavy responsibilities, his position is honorary and not compensated with money. On his retirement or death, he is succeeded by his assistant.

Besides the elders who handle social and political affairs are those who take care of matters of health. These chief diviners or medicine men are called *werkoi*. A *werkoion* is born, not appointed. He must be born with the art of healing and foretelling the future before he can

The *werkoion* works closely with the *kokwa* to decide what will benefit the community.

learn the necessary skills. It is the task of a *werkoion* to heal the sick, perform rituals, and read signals related to important future events.

In his role as soothsayer or prophet, the *werkoion* works closely with the *kokwa*. It is the *kokwa* that transmits the *werkoion's* recommendations to the community and decides what is to be done. As a medicine man, the *werkoion* is independent of the *kokwa* but works with an assistant. In his role as soothsayer he offers free communal service, but it is from his job as medicine man that he earns his living. Traditionally, he was paid in livestock, but today cash payments are sometimes acceptable.

With the introduction of Western-oriented cultures, foretelling the future is not as common

STORYTELLING

In a culture where writing is not used every day, storytelling is an important art form. The history and wisdom of a people must be remembered and retold. The young people must learn them and tell them to the next generation. Among the Pokot, like many other peoples of the world, good storytellers are respected as teachers, entertainers, and historians. The community depends on them to keep their culture alive.

A whole village may gather to hear stories and news, or a large group of children may have their wits tested with riddles and fables. The storyteller is called a *plakoion*, and he is expected to be a performer, as if on stage. He acts out the parts of the characters.

The stories are traditional, meaning that they are passed on from one person or generation to another. Therefore, most of a *plakoion*'s audience already know the story by heart. But the fun of hearing a traditional story is in the style and expression that a particular storyteller adds to it.

The listeners help the *plakoion* if he forgets an important detail. They chant encouragement to characters they like and boo the bad guys. Often there is a song in the middle of the story, and the whole audience sings along.

as it once was. However, the role of the *werkoion* as medicine man is still significant. Some illnesses are believed to respond better to customary medicine than to contemporary practices.▲

chapter

3

HISTORY

THE POKOT BELONG TO THE KENYAN ETHNIC group called the Kalenjin People. There are many theories on the origin of the Kalenjin, the most popular being a hot country north of Kenya, perhaps Sudan, Ethiopia, or Egypt. Kalenjin oral history refers to the country of origin as Emetab Burgei, which means "a hot country." They trekked along the Nile River as a united people. Eventually they settled around Tulwetab Kony (Mt. Elgon) between 500 and 1000 A.D.

Because of overpopulation, famine, disease, and other natural catastrophes, the Kalenjin People gradually split up and left the area around 1600. The Pokot initially settled on the northern side of Mt. Elgon and later spread north of Lake Baringo and the Cherangani Hills.

A Pokot woman builds a granary in which to store the season's harvest.

Typical granaries among the *pipapagh*, the agricultural Pokot.

▼ CHANGE OF DIRECTION ▼

The early part of the nineteenth century was a turning point in the history of the Pokot. They had lost most of their cattle to neighbors, the Maasai and the Nandi in particular. This drove them into adopting a new livelihood: farming. They grew corn, sorghum, and a grain called finger millet, so named because its stalks look like fingers. The Pokot borrowed irrigation methods from their neighbors the Marakwet. They farmed mainly along the Rivers Muruni and Weiwei. Thus, what they lost to some neighbors, they gained from others.

The cow is the most highly valued animal to the Pokot.

However, the Pokot never completely gave up their pastoral heritage. They still regarded animal husbandry as the most respectable means of livelihood, and cattle as an indispensable element in their lives. They were determined to own cattle once again.

▼ EXPANSION ▼
Around 1860 the Pokot raided the Samburu and Turkana peoples, seizing many cattle. Then they migrated and hid in the eastern part of the Chemongit Hills, where both farming and cattle-raising were possible.

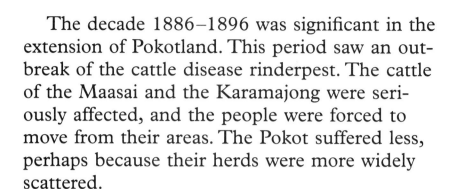

The decade 1886–1896 was significant in the extension of Pokotland. This period saw an outbreak of the cattle disease rinderpest. The cattle of the Maasai and the Karamajong were seriously affected, and the people were forced to move from their areas. The Pokot suffered less, perhaps because their herds were more widely scattered.

The outbreak of rinderpest had two results. First, the Pokot acquired the land left by the fleeing Maasai and Karamajong. Second, some of the Karamajong who had lost their cattle sought a new home among the Pokot. This led to a mixing of cultures. Some elements of the Karamajong language were taken into the Pokot language. But even more important, the Pokot borrowed from the Karamajong a system called *sarpan*, or the age-set system. The Pokot also started practicing circumcision, which is the first and most important step in the initiation of men into adulthood.

The early part of the twentieth century was difficult for the Pokot. It marked the beginning of colonial rule in Kenya. In addition to the demands of a foreign government, land was taken over by British settlers.▲

chapter

4

EUROPEAN CONTACT AND COLONIAL RULE

THE FIRST EUROPEANS BEGAN TO ARRIVE IN East Africa in the middle of the nineteenth century. By the turn of the twentieth century the British had begun to establish themselves in Pokotland. First they built a government station in the region. Then in 1913 there was talk of introducing new farming tools among the agricultural Pokot to encourage them to grow vegetables for sale at the station.

The Pokot watched the growth of European settlements around their homeland with increasing anxiety. They had heard how the new settlers had seized the land of neighboring peoples. They had also heard about the power of the white man's gun. Encouraged by their chief priest and elders to show restraint, the Pokot adopted a cautious attitude to the changes that were being introduced by the British settlers.

Young Pokot in full wardress. The shields are made of giraffe hide, and the cloaks are leopard skin.

A few years after the government station was established, a band of British soldiers seized land belonging to the Pokot in the Nzoia district and established farms for themselves. Shortly afterward, the colonial administration imposed a number of taxes on the Pokot. When their leaders protested, the government threatened to send in the King's African Rifles, a detachment of the British army, to quell the protests. To make the administration of the territory easier, headmen or chiefs were appointed by the government and their authority was forced on the people. Because the Pokot are a republican people, they resented the imposition of chiefs. But it quickly became clear that the British policy of colonization had begun.

Open resistance to European authority resulted. Led by Arimot, the chief priest of the pastoral Pokot, the entire country rose against colonial rule. Riots broke out across the countryside. The people scorned the British-appointed headmen and refused to recognize their authority to levy tax. In 1918, Arimot called for the overthrow of British rule. As prophet or *werkoion* of the Pokot, Arimot was also commander of the male age-sets. He quickly transformed the units into swift and able militias and undertook attacks to sabotage colonial interests.

The British District Commissioner in 1918,

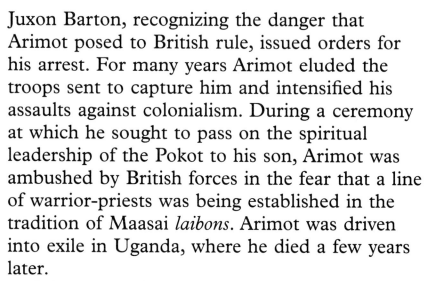

Juxon Barton, recognizing the danger that Arimot posed to British rule, issued orders for his arrest. For many years Arimot eluded the troops sent to capture him and intensified his assaults against colonialism. During a ceremony at which he sought to pass on the spiritual leadership of the Pokot to his son, Arimot was ambushed by British forces in the fear that a line of warrior-priests was being established in the tradition of Maasai *laibons*. Arimot was driven into exile in Uganda, where he died a few years later.

Arimot was the most respected and revered Pokot leader at the turn of the century. As *werkoion* or prophet he was honored by the Pokot as both a political crusader and a religious teacher. His death caused great bitterness against the British. European travelers to the region as late as 1950, thirty years after the event, reported that widespread anger was still expressed by the Pokot.

Pokot resistance to British rule gained force in the ensuing years. The Pokot refused to co-operate with the colonizers, and in return the British imposed heavier taxes and denied the people schools, hospitals, roads, and other facilities that were being developed in other parts of British East Africa. Ill-feeling continued to grow until the 1940s, when it erupted in a number of violent anti-European movements.

Pastoralist Pokot warriors. In the past, it was customary to tattoo their bodies with one scar for each enemy killed.

Increasing European settlement in Pokotland resulted in severe shortages of grazing land for the pastoralists. In an effort to control overgrazing, the government mandated that the Pokot sell a portion of their herds annually. This policy revealed remarkable ignorance of the significance of cattle in the life and religious beliefs of the Pokot. Violent protests occurred, particularly among the members of the male age-sets. There were renewed calls for the expulsion of the British from Pokotland. Many of the young men began to organize and formed a movement known as Dini ya Msambwa or "Spirit of the Ancestors."

The leader of Dini ya Msambwa was Lukas Pketch, a former pupil at the Roman Catholic school in West Suk. Pketch had become an embarrassment to the Catholic mission because of his calls for an end to colonial domination and the expulsion of British interests in the region. Membership swelled among disenchanted young Pokot men and women, and in 1948 the colonial authorities arrested Pketch. A year later he escaped from prison and organized a militia of Pokot warriors. In a skirmish with British troops, Pketch was killed along with eighteen of his men. District Officer Stevens and a number of other British officers also lost their lives.

A ruthless purge of Dini ya Msambwa was carried out by the colonial government. Although the movement reappeared in a number of guises in the years leading up to Kenyan independence, it never regained its initial force.

Kenya won independence in December 1963. The Pokot then came under African rule, which was nearly as restrictive as colonial rule. Nevertheless, the Pokot maintained their resolute, persevering character. They had to sustain their livelihood and maintain a social balance in their communities. The majority clung to their pastoral way of life despite the shortage of land. The 25 percent of the population who settled down to agriculture still kept a few cattle to supplement their income and to maintain their cultural heritage. The pastoralists and the agriculturalists continued to cement their relations through common beliefs and shared participation in social ceremonies and rituals.▲

chapter

5

CULTURE

THE POKOT BELIEVE IN THE EXISTENCE OF A supreme deity, Tororut. Their image of him is a huge, winged man. He is said to live up beyond the mountains, in the skies. He is very wealthy; that is, he has many cattle.

Tororut is all-powerful and all-knowing. He created the world and all the creatures in it, including human beings. It is up to him to decide whether these creatures will survive. Blessings such as the birth of children, the increase of cattle, or bumper harvests all come from him—as well as curses such as drought, famine, and disease. Tororut sends these natural catastrophes to punish human beings for committing various wrongs.

There are also lesser gods, who are really smaller parts of Tororut. On behalf of the

RELIGION

The Pokot believe that *onyet*, the human spirit, leaves the body after a person dies. The spirit then goes off to a cave or bush to be with the spirits of other ancestors. When a Pokot child is born, it is given the name of one of its ancestors. By calling out the name of a grandparent, for instance, the living can bring back the old spirit to live in the body of this new child. If the name of the spirit is not called out, the spirit becomes angry and brings bad luck to the child. The child is expected to look and act like its namesake.

The spirits of ancestors are powerful. If a person insults such spirits, he pays for it. Therefore, the Pokot take care to make the ancestors feel respected. They leave them tobacco or beer as gifts.

If a person does something terribly wrong, such as murder, the Pokot believe that he will be punished automatically. It is very frightening when anything upsets the ways of normal society. So, of course, anyone who behaves abnormally will be punished. This fear of supernatural punishment makes people behave with few laws or police.

Tororut, the Pokot deity, can bring both good and bad luck. He punishes people when they misbehave or fail to take care of their families. For example, a man who mistreats his cattle angers Tororut.

The Pokot believe in divination and soothsaying, that is, the ability to tell the future. Everyone knows how to do a little fortune-telling. And everyone has the ability to curse by calling on Tororut and using sacred objects.

Diviners, who are believed to have the power to kill with curses, are greatly feared. If a person begins acting strangely, people may think that he is practicing witchcraft. Sometimes even animals are thought to be sorcerers, if they behave in strange ways.

supreme deity, they perform various functions in the daily lives of the Pokot.

The most important of the smaller deities are Asis, the sun, and Ilat, thunder. In fact, when the Pokot pray, it is to Asis and Ilat, who act as messengers between Tororut and the people.

The sun is seen as both good and evil. Its power affects events in people's lives. It is the protector, especially of women and children. On the other hand, the sun is thought to cause drought when people have offended Tororut. When a Pokot wants to bless someone, he says, for example, "May the sun smile upon you." But the sun is also invoked as a curse. The worst curse is, "May the sun kill you."

Thunder is both respected and feared. Ilat is believed to be very powerful. Its noise instills fear. The way thunder brings rain creates an air of mystery around it. The Pokot view rain as a blessing from Tororut showered to them through Ilat as his messenger.

Still smaller gods are Arawa, the moon, Kokel, the stars, and Tapogh, the evening star. Arawa guides the Pokot in telling the months of the year. The stars help to forecast rain. From the position of Tapogh for example, they can estimate when the rainy season will begin so that they can start planting at the right time.

Religion is part of the daily lives of the Pokot. Prayers are said, for example, at the beginning of a ritual or ceremony to invoke the super-

A Pokot bride is not considered truly married until she has a child.

natural powers. The aim is to ward off evil and ensure good luck and success.

Rituals and ceremonies attend many situations in the lives of the Pokot. Through ritual, the gods are asked for assistance. Ritual helps the Pokot maintain good relations within the community and come to terms with their impoverished environment.

Elements of ritual are involved in settling disputes. A dispute is heard at a meeting called a *kiruok*, chaired by the most powerful elder, the *kiruokintin*. Prayers are said by two elders, one representing the injured party and the other representing the accused. In traditional prayers and incantations, the elders ask the gods for peace and for punishment of any evil person.

If the accused is found guilty, the elders decide on his punishment and announce it publicly. If the person still claims to be innocent, he is subjected to ritual "oathing"; his accusers swear that the gods will punish him should they find him guilty. For example, the accused can consume a specially prepared concoction and swear that if he is guilty the mixture will kill him. If he is guilty, he is supposed to die within a prescribed period.

When a serious crime such as murder has been committed, ritual prayers are used to force the culprit to confess. The elders perform communal cursing, threatening the guilty person with some specified punishment. Such a curse is greatly feared. Often the culprit would rather confess than face the consequences of the curse.

Foretelling the future and practicing customary medicine both depend on ritual. The *werkoion*, the chief diviner or medicine man, decides what ingredients to use for a cure. These items, such as a goat of a certain color, depend on the nature of the task or illness involved. The *werkoion* calls on the supernatural powers to help him in his work.

▼ RITES OF PASSAGE ▼

Birth, initiation, wedding, and death are marked by special rituals and ceremonies. Each of these events concerns the whole community.

The **birth** of a child is a very important event. A bride is not regarded as a truly married woman until she has given birth to her first child. Her first duty is to produce children for her husband. A man who does not have children is exiled by the community. If a woman does not produce children for her husband, she must leave. Children, particularly boys, give the Pokot assurance that their clans and their people as a whole will continue. Children are the support of their parents in old age.

During pregnancy, a woman receives great care to ensure the health of the expected baby. She is given milk from a cow that has never been sick. A pregnant woman must never see a monkey, an occurrence believed to cause deformity in the unborn baby.

At the birth of the child, Tororut is invoked to bless the baby with health and strength. Women sing and dance. The dances performed depend on the sex of the newborn: A boy is received with greater enthusiasm than a girl.

The birth of a woman's first child is celebrated in a ceremony known as *parpara*. Clan members of both the father and mother participate. On the eve of the ceremony the expectant

While in seclusion, the girls are *chemeri*, neither girls nor women. If they leave the hut, they must cover their face with white chalk to identify them to the rest of the community.

After the seclusion hut is ritually cleansed, it is abandoned.

The mothers of *chemeri* perform a dance as part of the initiation rituals.

mother confesses any wrong she may have committed that could interfere with the birth of the baby. During the ceremony, as the participants drink, the mother undergoes ritual cleansing. The purpose of *parpara* is to purify new parents and to ward off evil from the baby.

Many Pokot practice initiation rites. Because of cultural interaction with other ethnic groups, not all Pokot participate in the rite, but those who do practice it are in the majority.

Initiation marks the end of childhood and entry into adulthood. For girls, the rite is performed at about thirteen years of age; for boys, between fifteen and twenty years old.

The circumcision period is a season of celebration and joy for a whole community. It is marked by feasting, singing, and dancing. Satirical songs are sung to remind people of the moral code. As they dance, the people ease pent-up emotions and rebuild their sense of brotherhood. The experience reminds the Pokot that they are one community, one people. Prayers are said to invoke Tororut for blessings. Ritual cleansing is performed to ward off evil and to ensure that the initiates move successfully from childhood to adulthood.

During their initiation, the girls are secluded in a hut built for the purpose. It is taboo for anyone other than the girls and their caretakers to enter the hut. After the seclusion period, the hut is ritually cleansed, then abandoned.

Boys prepare to become warriors as well as men when they enter initiation.

While in seclusion, the girls are *chemeri*, initiates who are neither children nor adults. If they go outside the hut they must cover their face with white chalk to identify themselves. The girls remain in seclusion for two to three months, during which they are very well fed and their health is attended to by special women. More important, they are taught the role of a wife, including sex education.

At the end of the seclusion period, the girls discard the wooden beads they have been wearing. This act is symbolic of leaving childhood behind. They are now adult women ready for marriage.

The boys' initiation ceremony is not only into adulthood; they are also preparing to become warriors. For this reason, male initiation includes ordeals to test bravery and courage. The boys are also expected to show bravery by not flinching during the circumcision.

After circumcision, the boys are secluded in a hut called *mencha* for four or five months. There

At *sapana*, the climax of initiation, there is much celebration.

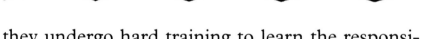

they undergo hard training to learn the responsibilities of a husband and a warrior.

At the end of the seclusion period, the *kipuno*
is held. This ceremony is both a ritual and a
social celebration. The whole community joins
in feasting, singing, and dancing. The young
men discard their childhood names and take on
permanent ones.

Kipuno culminates in the assigning of an age-
set to the new group of men, to which they will
belong for the rest of their lives. The Pokot have
seven age-sets, the name given to a group of
men. Each member is committed to protect
the other members of his set and the whole
community.

Following the *kipuno* is an interim period
during which each man prepares for his final
independence from his mother's hut. He is given
assistance in building his own hut.

The climax of initiation, *sapana*, is the recep-
tion for the young men who have shed childhood. They are now are known as *muran*,
warriors. They wear the clay headdress as part
of their new identity. They are also ready for
marriage.

Among the Pokot, **marriage** is an important
event in life. It is in marriage that a man proves
his manhood and a woman her womanhood by
producing children.

Although young people can decide to run

away together, the most acceptable form of marriage is through negotiation. A young man woos a girl either at dances or when she is performing her daily chores. When he has decided that he wants to marry her, he and his male friends take a gift of beer to the girl's father. If the father accepts the beer, it means he accepts the young man as his future son-in-law.

The next step is for the clan elders on either side to negotiate. The elders on the young man's side trace the history of the girl's ancestors to determine whether she is an appropriate wife for him. It is important, for example, to know whether her clan produces men of worth. The negotiations then move to the bridewealth, a payment of cattle that the young man must make to the father of his bride. The two sides argue until they reach agreement on the number of livestock to be paid.

After payment of dowry, the *nosia*, a wedding ceremony, is held. The *nosia* is held in the young man's homestead, but it is a day of celebration for the whole neighborhood. The bride and groom stand side by side in the middle of the compound. A wedding band made of leather is fastened on the girl's right wrist. Prayers are said asking for blessings. After this serious part of the ceremony, the community celebrates the occasion by drinking, singing, and dancing. The wedding songs are designed to remind everyone what is expected of them. Men are reminded of their responsibilities toward their wives, and wives also receive their share of reminders.

Funerals are not common among the Pokot. The Pokot fear death. In the traditional days, poor people, children, and young people without children were simply thrown into the bush when they died. It was taboo to talk about a dead person.

A funeral ceremony is held for an old wealthy man. His children, relatives, neighbors, and friends mourn him. He is buried near his homestead. Ritual is performed to cleanse the entire household. Four days after the burial a more public ceremony may be performed.

▼ EDUCATION ▼

Before the introduction of Western education, the Pokot had their own methods of teaching youth to be responsible people. The training involved the use of oral literature or folklore: stories, songs, proverbs, and riddles.

Most of the stories told to children contain specific morals. The stories are told in a humorous manner to entertain the children while making the message clear.

Songs occur in some stories and serve as additional teaching devices. Other songs are used at ceremonies, dances, or even at work. In Pokot, the songs teach by biting humor; the message is given indirectly but in a sharp, sarcastic manner. The education gained through songs is not limited to children; adults are also reminded of expected moral behavior.

Like songs, proverbs are used with versatility. They are quoted at public meetings and even at the deliberations of the elders when they are settling disputes. Here their purpose is not to teach but to illustrate points. A person may use proverbs to show what a good speaker he is. Verbal art is very important among the Pokot. Proverbs are used frequently to shame youths for bad behavior and warn them of the consequences of straying from the moral path.

Riddles are used mostly for children. At storytelling sessions, the narrator poses a number of riddles to sharpen their wits or capture their attention. Children use riddles among themselves at play. Riddles can also be used to teach children about their community and the world around them.

Even with the introduction of Western education, the Pokot still use folklore as a means of teaching. Its strength lies in the fact that it is a way to keep the culture alive.

▼ THE PLACE OF CATTLE ▼

Livestock, particularly cattle, have occupied a central position in the culture of the Pokot for many generations. Even those who have become

POKOT RIDDLES

Who am I?

Q: *Reo-e' ti'-chu lopai pirir kirokit.*
A: *Kelat ngo ngaliep.*

Q: My cows are white, my bull is red.
A: Teeth and tongue.

Q: *Kolimanan ato-ocha loh.*
A: *Kadongut.*

Q: I can be heard even very far away.
A: A cowbell.

Q: *Kopa' setapoh ka-maiyitan.*
A: *Krisio.*

Q: I carried water and did not spill any.
A: A cow's udder.

Q: *Ocha kogh maminye.*
A: *Or.*

Q: There is no one longer than I.
A: A road.

Q: *Kowuita' minyon to cheptoya.*
A: *Yim.*

Q: I am the stretched skin of a dark ox.
A: The night sky.

Q: *Ocha pertat maminye chi nyanyuruacha.*
A: *Konyen.*

Q: We are so swift that no man can catch us.
A: Eyes.

agriculturalists keep one or two cows to maintain pastoral traditions. A Pokot man who has no cattle is regarded as poor even if he has other material possessions.

Before the Pokot began using money, livestock served as currency. In trading negotiations, an item was valued at so many cows and so many goats or sheep. Grazing land or farmland was also valued in this way. Cattle played a crucial role in marriages. A Pokot man who wants to marry still needs to pay cattle to his future father-in-law as bridewealth.

Cattle ownership is also a mark of prestige. A man's social standing depends on the size of his herd.

Cattle ownership cements relationships. People make cattle-use agreements, which are formal exchanges of a cow for a steer. A person who needs a steer in his herd can give one of his cows to another man in return for a steer. The owner of the cow is then entitled to half of the calves his cow produces. The association thus formed between the two men is known as *tilia*.

Cattle are considered beautiful. A woman may be described as beautiful as a cow. Steers in particular are regarded as handsome. It is common for a man to have a favorite steer that he treats as a pet. Even when such a steer grows old, the owner would rather give it to a friend than slaughter it. The Pokot often give cattle pet names and compose praise songs for them. A praise song to a steer is composed over many years, changing a little each time it is sung. A young man may take the name of his father's favorite steer when he discards his childhood name at initiation.▲

chapter

6

DAILY LIFE

EACH PERSON IN A POKOT COMMUNITY HAS A specific role to play in the family's daily life. The activities are assigned according to age and sex.

The Pokot rear zebu cattle, goats, and some sheep. Modern breeds of cattle are gradually being introduced. Men herd the cattle, often helped by children. It is also the job of men to break virgin land for cultivation. Men attend public meetings to run the affairs of families and of the community at large. In olden times young *muran* or warriors went to war to defend their communities against enemy ethnic groups. Today the work of the *muran* is to provide general security for their neighborhoods.

In both farming and animal husbandry, women's contribution is tremendous. It is women who cultivate, plant, weed, and harvest the crops. The building of houses is also women's work. Milking cows is done only by women. It is considered similar to providing milk for children, which only women can do. A man who milks a cow is said to be "acting like a woman." The utensils for milking and storing milk are made and cleaned by women. All activities related to preparing food are the responsibility of women, except for the slaughtering of animals and sharing the meat. That is men's work and is taboo for a woman.

In some areas of Pokotland, production of honey is practiced. Men are the beekeepers. They carve hives or *moghen* from tree trunks. They also make huge hide bags called *tokogh* for collecting the honey.

Pokotland has artisans: blacksmiths, wood-carvers, potters, weavers, and people skilled in body decorating and making ornaments. Black-smiths are often people who do not own a single cow. The Pokot say of blacksmiths that since Tororut refused to give them livestock, he gave them in compensation the intelligence to prac-tice a craft. Women are forbidden to watch a blacksmith at work. It is believed that if a woman sees a blacksmith working, his equip-ment will become heavy in his hand, and he will go insane.

Pottery is the secret of women artists. Young women and girls may not see the operation. It is believed that if a man sees a pot before it is

The arts of body makeup and ornamentation are of great importance
among the Pokot.

finished, it will break within a month; if a man
steps over a pot, he will die within a year.

Weaving is also done by women. They use
straw to make baskets of various sizes and
uses. The most beautiful baskets are small food
carriers called *karop*, so finely woven that they
could hold water. Unlike smithing and pottery,
weaving is not a secret art. It is a task that a
woman can perform while conversing with
others and even while walking to market.

52   Other household articles made by women

The Pokot dance at ceremonial feasts and at social gatherings. Like many peoples in Africa, they dance in groups and usually in a circle. Often the dancing consists of moving sidewise in the circle while stamping the feet in rhythm and moving the hips and shoulders. Rhythm is more important than music in this kind of dancing.

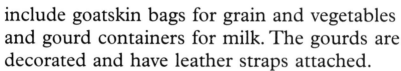

include goatskin bags for grain and vegetables and gourd containers for milk. The gourds are decorated and have leather straps attached.

Woodcarving is a very useful art among the Pokot. Men make such objects as hoeheads, wooden trays, and bowls. They also carve wooden headrests called *ngachar*. Almost every Pokot elder owns a *ngachar*, which he uses as a seat or headrest.

The Pokot are very concerned with their physical appearance. Hence the arts of body makeup and ornamentation are of great importance. Both male and female artists practice this art. Beadwork is done mainly by women. They make necklaces, headbands, wristbands, and earrings for both men and women. Shiny metal coils worn by women on the neck and wrists and above the elbow are fixed on the body of the wearer by male specialists. Men make decorative headdresses with the skin of colobus monkeys and ostrich feathers. Both men and women practice body scarification, the art of decorating the skin by making scars in patterns. The full glamour of Pokot body makeup can be appreciated at a traditional dance, when every dancer shows off his or her best.▲

chapter

7

A VIEW OF THE FUTURE

CULTURE IS NOT STATIC, BUT HAS THE
potential to adapt to changing circumstances.
New ways of life are introduced through political
or economic events, through changes in the
environment, or through interaction with people
of different cultures. In this same vein the Pokot
culture is not static; it is open to new influences.

As mentioned earlier, British colonial rule
was introduced in Kenya during the late nineteenth and early twentieth centuries. The
colonizers brought new cultural elements with
them, including a central government, formal
education, new kinds of medicines and hospitals,
new legal systems, individual land ownership,
and new agricultural and pastoral methods.

Although at first the Pokot strongly resisted
change, gradually they have modified some of
their traditions. It must be noted, however, that

Many changes have affected the day-to-day life of the Pokot, and indeed, all the peoples of Kenya. Many have had to find jobs for wages in cities like Nairobi.

the Pokot have experienced problems in adapting to new situations and assimilating new cultural elements.

Pastoral life has presented the greatest problems. A major reason for this is the conflict between the way the Pokot have thought of the land and the way modern governments think of it. Traditionally, pastoral land was owned by everyone in the community. No one person owned any piece of land. Pastureland had no boundaries. This made it possible for the Pokot to roam far and wide until they found greener pastures and water for their cattle. Today all the land is owned either by the government or by rich ranchers. The Pokot cannot let their cattle graze freely without being charged with trespassing.

Another major area of conflict between the old and the new is in the raising of livestock. Traditionally the Pokot reared zebu, a breed of cattle that survives well in their rough land. However, zebu do not provide high-quality meat, and they produce little milk. The government has encouraged the Pokot to rear new breeds of cattle and to keep smaller herds. The Pokot understand the reasons for these proposals, but they conflict with Pokot traditions. As we have seen, a man's prestige and social standing are judged by the size of his herd; the quality of the herd is not important. The relationship between Pokot and their cattle is also an issue. A Pokot's emotional attachment to his animals makes it difficult for him to get rid of them wholesale and replace them with a few so-called better breeds.

New agricultural and pastoral methods cannot be effectively introduced without first creating the necessary facilities. Pokotland is semiarid. The new breeds of cattle cannot survive in the pasture conditions in which zebu thrive. That means that boreholes and other modern facilities must be built to provide enough water.

All these changes and many others of the past

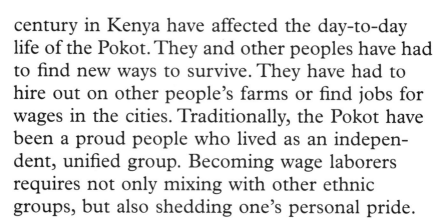

century in Kenya have affected the day-to-day life of the Pokot. They and other peoples have had to find new ways to survive. They have had to hire out on other people's farms or find jobs for wages in the cities. Traditionally, the Pokot have been a proud people who lived as an independent, unified group. Becoming wage laborers requires not only mixing with other ethnic groups, but also shedding one's personal pride.

But the situation is not as gloomy as it may sound. Attempts have been made to improve the condition of the land. Government programs are trying to help people adapt to the changing situation and still maintain their identity.

Schools have been built; however, cultural, economic, and other practical problems combine to produce low enrollment. Medical centers have also been built, but problems of transportation and communication make it difficult for much of the population to use them.

The current government of Kenya is committed to assisting the Pokot and other Kenyan peoples affected by the results of colonialism. The few educated Pokot are also interested in improving the quality of life of their people. It is hoped that as they attempt to adapt their land and life-styles to the demands of the modern world, the Pokot will preserve those values that contribute to the warmth and brotherhood of their people.▲

Glossary

age-sets Groups into which men are divided when they are initiated.

agriculturalists People who make their living by farming.

bridewealth The number of cattle a young man must pay to the father of the woman he wants to marry.

divination Foretelling the future.

initiation Training period and ceremonies by which boys and girls pass into adulthood.

Kalenjin Group of seven peoples near Lake Victoria in Kenya, speaking related languages.

kipuno Feasting ceremony during initiation when boys give up their childhood names and take adult ones.

kiruokintin The chief elder in charge of settling disputes in the community.

kokwa The group of elders who make decisions and laws for a village.

muran (warriors) Young men after initiation.

nosia Pokot wedding ceremony.

parpara Ceremony celebrating the birth of a woman's first child.

pastoralists People who make a living by raising cattle.

pipapagh "Grain people," the Pokot name for agriculturalists.

pipatich "Cattle people," the Pokot name for pastoralists.

poion The elder at the head of each Pokot homestead.

sapana Final initiation ceremony, when boys become warriors (*muran*).

Suk Another name for the Pokot people and their language.

taboo An act that is forbidden because it is believed to bring bad luck.

Tororut The Pokot deity.

totem An animal that represents and protects each clan within an ethnic group.

werkoion A foreteller of the future and healer.

zebu Sturdy cattle that thrive in the rough climate of Kenya.

For Further Reading

Beech, Mervyn W.H. *The Suk: Their Language and Folklore.* London: Oxford University Press, 1911.

Chesaina, C. *Oral Literature of the Kalenjin.* Nairobi: Heinemann, 1991.

Boyd, Herb. *African History for Beginners: Part 1—Africa Dawn, A Diasporan View.* New York: Writers and Readers, 1991.

Clark, Leon E. *Through African Eyes: The Past Road to Independence,* rev. ed. New York: Center for International Training and Education, 1991.

Garlake, Peter. *The Kingdoms of Africa,* rev. ed. New York: Peter Berick Books, 1990.

Half-Dozen Traditional Songs of Kenya Series. Book 2. Nairobi: Sol-Fa Music Enterprises, 1973.

Hennings, Richard Owen. *African Morning.* London: Chatto & Windus, 1951.

Kipkorir, Benjamin, and Welbourn, F.B. *The Marakwet of Kenya.* Nairobi: East African Publishing House, 1973.

Lamb, David. *The Africans.* New York: Random House, 1987.

Moss, Joyce, and Wilson, George. *People of the World: Africans South of the Sahara.* Detroit: Gale Research Inc., 1991.

Were, Gideon S. *Western Kenya Historial Texts.* Nairobi: East African Literature Bureau, 1967.

Were, Gideon, and Wilson, D.A. *East Africa Through a Thousand Years,* rev. ed. London: Evans Brothers, 1972.

Index

ABOUT THE AUTHOR

Professor Ciarunji Chesaina Swinimer holds a B.A. degree in English and French, an M.Ed. in Child Psychology, an M.A. in Literature, and a Ph.D. in Literature. Besides having taught literature for over twenty years, and currently at the University of Nairobi, she is interested in women's studies and has published two papers in this field. Prof. Swinimer has also published three books, including *Oral Literature of the Kalenjin*. She sits on several national committees, including the Kenya English Panel and the Humanities and Social Sciences Committee of the Kenya National Academy of Sciences.

PHOTO CREDITS:

Cover Photo: Herbert M. Cole
AP/Wide World (p. 56); CFM, Nairobi (all other photos)

PHOTO RESEARCH:

Vera Ahmadzadeh with Jennifer Croft

DESIGN:

Kim Sonsky